W9-CIN-270

HOW TO PRESERVE ANIMAL AND OTHER SPECIMENS IN CLEAR PLASTIC

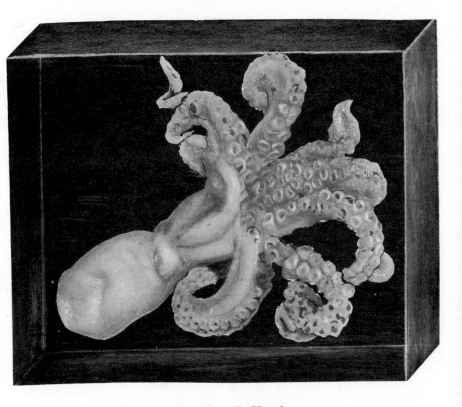

By Cleo E. Harden

Illustrated by David G. Harden

Edited by Vinson Brown

Copyright, 1963, by Cleo E. Harden

Paper Edition: ISBN 0-911010-46-7
Cloth Edition: ISBN 0-911010-47-5

Naturegraph Publishers, Inc., Happy Camp, California 96039

HOUSTON PUBLIC LIBRARY

2

RO1436554496
SSC

TABLE OF CONTENTS

SPECIAL WARNING

Various solutions and chemicals are used in the preparation of plastic mounts that may be harmful to smell or to leave on the skin. Precautions should be taken not to inhale such things as chloroform, ether and formalin, and hands should be thoroughly washed in soap and water after using fixing solutions, etc. Particular precautions should be taken not to allow children or uninformed persons to use or touch any of these things, and all dangerous chemicals or solutions should be kept in a safe place out of the reach of the hands of children. Special permission may be necessary to obtain some chemicals, such as ethyl alcohol. See your nearest biology laboratory about this.

ILLUSTRATIONS

ACKNOWLEDGMENTS

The author would like to take this opportunity to thank all of those people who have given their time and encouragement during the preparation of this book. He is especially indebted to the following:

Dr. Joel Hedgpeth for his advice, cooperation and kind consideration in allowing some of the research for the book to be carried on under his direction at the Pacific Marine Station of the University of the Pacific at Dillon Beach, California.

Dr. Karl Lang, Supervisor for the Department of Invertebrates, Swedish State Museum of Natural History, Stockholm, Sweden, for reading the manuscript and making worthwhile suggestions for its revision.

Earnest L. Lutz and Natcol Laboratories for their advice and permission to use some of the vital data from their publication, Plastic Embedding and Laminating with NL600 Series Resins.

Jonie Lewis and Pauline Harden for reading and correcting the first draft of the paper and for their suggestions and encouragements.

David G. Harden for working with me on many of the experiments which established the techniques as they are printed, and for his fine group of illustrations.

CORRECTIONS, PROBLEMS & SOLUTIONS

The preservation of natural-looking study specimens has long been the desire of great natural history teachers throughout the world. Robert Hooke, curator of the British Museum in 1782, states that an all time objective of naturalists is to have a collection of "natural bodies" assembled in "as full and complete a collection of all varieties ... as could be obtained, where an inquirer might ... pause, and turn over, and spell, and read the book of nature, and observe ... nature's grammar, and by which, as with a dictionary, he might readily turn to find the true figure, composition, derivation, and the use of characters, words, phrases and sentences of nature written with indelible, and most exact, and most expressive letters, without which book it will be very difficult to be thoroughly a literatus in the language and sense of nature. The use of such a collection is not for divertisements, wonders and gazing, as it is for the most part thought and esteemed, and like a picture for children to admire and be pleased with, but for the serious and diligent study of the most able" ... scientists.

The earliest records of attempts to preserve study specimens indicate that it had its rise along with the study of human anatomy. It was through a long line of trial and error techniques and experimentation that our modern methods have been derived. Original dissections for the study of human anatomy were made on unpreserved bodies. Most of these dissections were made within a three day period, during which time the investigators worked both day and night in order that they might complete the task before putrefaction made working conditions impossible. Versalius (1537-42) described the female generative organs in De Humani Corpis Fabrica, based on a study of six bodies, of which only one was dissected under reasonably good conditions. Soon afterward he prepared the oldest existing skeleton and presented it to the University of Basle in 1546. Liquid preservatives were not discovered until about 1660, so bones, ligaments and hard tissues attracted most of the early attention.

Robert Boyle is credited with the discovery of the preserving qualities of wine. This information was included in a report at the Royal Society Meeting in London in 1662 when Mr. Crowne presented the society with two puppies preserved in this medium. Liquid preservatives made injections possible and great strides were made by the end of the seventeenth century.

It was not until 1893 that formalin came into use. Blum first recommended its use and Eccles, in 1894, presented a technique whereby specimens preserved in formalin and then dipped in alcohol before storing, returned to a state of natural color.* This, however, did not solve the problem of preserving pigments. Color preservation of these early anatomists was mainly concerned with the retention of the red color of haematin and was not involved in the multiple problems of surface pigments of gross specimens.

Liquid preservatives and their development established the use of wet preparations for museum study specimens. Such specimens are employed today for serious study in all of the branches of biological science. They are indispensable in comparative studies of both external and anatomical characteristics of both plants and animals. There is no doubt that they will remain with us even though the advancement in new polyester resin techniques offer many advantages in areas where excessive abuse might be disastrous to the more delicate museum jar preparations.

Plastic as a medium for mounting zoological and botanical specimens for study and display purposes has endless possibilities. Its clarity and ease of handling, even to use under low power magnification are far superior to the museum jar. Its permanency has not yet been determined, but Natcol Products Company have a display of butterflies which has been exposed to sunlight for five years and which show no apparent signs of deterioration. During this study four separate mounts of female <u>Pagurus</u>, hermit crabs, with eggs attached, were exposed to direct sunlight in temperatures which ranged daily from 90 degrees F to 110 degrees F and over a two months period. No change in the specimens was noticed although there was a slight fading in the photographic name tag that was embedded with the specimens. Flowers and botanical specimens have likewise been successfully embedded in full color without fading. (Dr. Randolph Sprecht, <u>Preservation of Color and Shape in Flowers</u>, Bulletin Series No. 40, College of Engineering, University of Florida, Gainesville, Florida.) In fact, there is no indication that

---

*Jores, 1913: The action of formalin, supported by the presence of alkaline salts, transforms the blood coloring into acid haematin. Further treatment of the specimen with alcohol transforms the acid haematin to alkaline haematin which has a color similar to haemoglobin (blood pigment).

 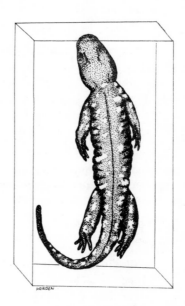

PLATE 1. <u>Two Types of Mounts</u>. The specimen of a fetal shark on left compared with a plastic mount of a salamander on right may help the reader to understand some of the advantages and disadvantages of both types of mount. Although the plastic block gives an undistorted view of external characteristics, it does not offer the advantage of close probing. The liquid in most museum-jar specimens requires frequent changes and continual replenishment.

---

specimens prepared in this medium will ever fade or deteriorate once they are successfully embedded in the crystal clear block.

It is true, however, that a specimen once mounted, is trapped inside its transparent case and can never be removed for close examination and probing such as might be done with a specimen within a fluid medium. Possibly these mounts should supplement rather than replace the museum jar. An account is told, in the County Schools Office of Fresno County, California, of an attempt to remove arrowheads from plastic resin mounts by dissolving the plastic in acetone and other solvents. This attempt was reported to be a complete failure since the removal of the strain within the block set up such a stress in the stone pieces that they were shattered by the internal pressure.   No successful method, as yet, has been found to dissolve these resins when polymerization is complete.

It is not hard to realize that this new medium has both advantages and disadvantages.   Its usefulness, however, is not questioned in cases where rough handling is expected.

Plastic mounted specimens may be purchased from some of the biological supply houses, such as: General Biological Supply House, Inc. (Turtox), Stansi Scientific Company, Ward's Natural Science Establishment, and others.

Many collectors are mounting or have attempted to mount their own specimens in plastic. Some have had fair success while others have given up after encountering some of the unforseen difficulties.

Some of the problems encountered by those who have tried to embed specimens are as follows:

1.   Available literature on successful procedures has been limited and fragmentary.
2.   The procedures which have been published have not taken into account differences in protoplasmic structures which require   a modification of techniques.
3.   Color, an important factor in good mounting, lacks sufficient research.
4.   Special techniques for clearing, differential staining, injection, dissection and so on have not been generally discussed.
5.   Grinding and polishing of the finished blocks has required the installation of special, expensive equipment.   When the same work is attempted without such equipment, it is usually unsatisfactory and very time consuming.
6.   Commercial resins, although much alike in their   finished appearance, are made up by different formulas and have variable characteristics. Some develop extreme internal temperatures that thoroughly cook the specimens, while others require curing ovens to complete polymerization.   It is extremely important for the operator to become acquainted with these differences and to select a resin that will insure constant results.

It is intended that this book will provide answers to some of these problems. The information presented is the result of experimentation and research which has provided many beautiful mounts and it is the author's desire that such information will bring success to others. Added objectives of this book will be:

1. To distinguish between types of specimens and to choose the proper procedure for preserving, dehydrating and mounting.

2. To describe procedures and techniques which have been applied and which have proven themselves through repeated experimentation.

3. To suggest further experimentation which might increase the present scope of embedding and to encourage others to further explore this field.

4. To stimulate the imagination of good teachers in the use of plastic mounts as a practical teaching aid.

5. To suggest a new method of molding polished blocks, thus eliminating the necessity of special machinery for grinding and polishing. This technique, when applied with self setting and hardening plastics will also eliminate the use of ovens or any other bulky, expensive equipment. This should make it practical to produce fine specimens in the average school laboratory.

6. To encourage students to use plastic mounts for the preservation of extraordinary specimens within their field of study.

The bibliography will include few books. Reliable information on plastic embedding of "wet" specimens is limited. Most of the published materials have appeared as single articles in magazines of scientific appeal. It is suggested that those interested in carrying on further research should keep in touch with articles that occasionally appear in current periodicals.

It has been found that many of the micrological techniques published in various texts may be applied to plastic mounting. This is especially true of general procedures in regard to dyeing and staining of tissue or gross specimens. Injected and dissected specimens can also be mounted with slight modification of standard micrological procedures.

Although some mention of plants may be made, this paper will deal principally with animals. For the botanist the bulletin mentioned on page 4 is available through the University of Florida.

"Embedding and Laminating" by Earnest L. Lutz and published by Natcol Products Company, P. O. Box 227, Redlands, California, covers a number of techniques for both the botanist and the zoologist. Permission has been granted by Mr. Lutz and the Natcol Products Company to include some basic information from this manual.

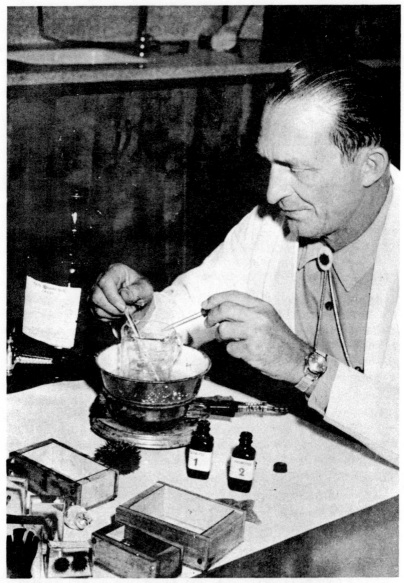

PLATE 2.   The Author Working in the School Laboratory.
The research for techniques described in this text was done in a
high school laboratory and without the advantage of any special
equipment.

MATERIALS AND EQUIPMENT

1. Resins used for embedding "wet" or "dry" specimens for biological purposes are sold under various trade names and are shipped in liquid state. The liquid is about the consistency of strained honey and varies in shade from light yellow to a deep straw yellow. Variabilities in these resins are due to the formula of the manufacturer. Since they are organic substances composed of molecules of the carbon compounds which, being compatible with each other, will polymerize under the proper conditions, the variety of combinations are many and it is likely that no two resins are of identical composition.

During the process of polymerization the molecules arrange themselves in chains. The chains, being slightly more compact, settle to the bottom and rearrange themselves by hooking to other short chains. Cross-linkage between the chains takes place to eventually produce a solid block. Catalysts are used to control the speed of polymerization and these are shipped in separate containers to be added to the liquid plastic at the time of use. There are usually two catalysts, one which brings about gelling of the medium in a short time and the other which sets up the final linkage. Some heat within the block is required for final curing and this is usually developed within the resin itself since the chemical reaction is exothermic. In some of the resins developed by manufacturers catalysts have been added to reduce the amount of heat produced. In this case it is necessary to bake the block at a controlled temperature to bring about final linkage of molecules.

In those plastics which are entirely self-setting the speed of the exothermic reaction and the amount of heat produced are controlled by the amount and kind of catalysts added to the liquid resin both during the manufacturing process and at the time the resin is used. Each manufacturer includes information concerning the amount of each catalyst to use with his shipment of resin. This usually includes a series of formulas for mixing slow-setting, medium-setting, fast-setting and sometimes very fast-setting batches. It is usually a good idea to mix a small amount of resin according to one of the formulas and check the speed prior to the actual use of the resin. Under normal conditions a formula should be chosen which will produce a solid block within twenty-four to forty-eight hours. Room temperature and possibly humidity may cause a great variation in curing time. Overheating caused by the use of too much catalyst

may be disastrous to both the specimen and block. If too little catalyst is used, some trouble may be encountered in getting the plastic to set in a reasonable time.

2. Plastic resins are incompatible with water. This has important implications when dealing with biological specimens which are
of extremely high water content. During the exothermic reaction
mentioned earlier, any water in the tissue may be turned to steam.
If the steam pressure is great enough inside the block, it may cause
it to crack (see Plate 3).

PLATE 3. <u>Cracked Block.</u> - A cracked block and shriveled
specimen is usually the result of too much heat during the curing
process. This may be prevented by using less catalyst or by reducing the temperature of the curing room.

Note also the air bubbles that were caught by the quick-setting
plastic.

If the steam pressure is only slight, mainly within the tissue
itself, it will force the water molecules through the lattice structure of the plastic in such a manner that white opaque areas develop. Such areas obstruct viewing the specimen and make it
unsightly. (See Plate 4 on next page.) A poorly dehydrated animal
may be entirely shrouded with this opaque structure. "Wet" specimens must have all water removed from the tissue if successful embedding is to be accomplished.

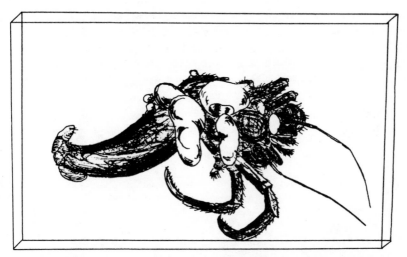

PLATE 4. <u>Hermit Crab with White Opaque Areas.</u> - It is extremely important to have all water removed from an animal before embedding. The white areas caused by moisture make the mount unattractive and likewise obstruct the view of the specimen.

3. A general outline of the procedure used to embed "wet" specimens is as follows:
   a. Cure and preserve the animal.
   b. Dehydrate the tissues by replacement of the water or other liquids with substances compatible with the resin.
   c. Infiltrate plastic into the tissue to replace the dehydrating agent.
   d. Embed in catalyzed plastic.

WET AND DRY SPECIMENS

4. Some specimens are considered as dry. These are relatively simple to embed. Dry specimens include those things which contain little or no water. However, since oils, which are also present, may present special problems, it is best to consider a dry specimen as one that is relatively free of both water and oil. Sea shells, mineral samples, crystals, fossils and dry plants are representative of this group. (See examples in Plate 5 on page 14.) Seeds, dried chitinous insects, pine cones, etc., should be considered as oily and should be immersed in acetone or ether a few minutes before

embedding. They should then be removed from the solvent and re-dried on tissue paper before mounting. Wet specimens all require special techniques that will be described later.   They include all animals with any moisture in their bodies (see Plate 6, below).

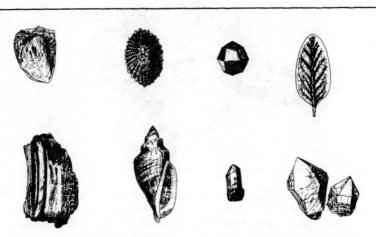

PLATE 5. Typical "Dry Specimens", as described on page 13.

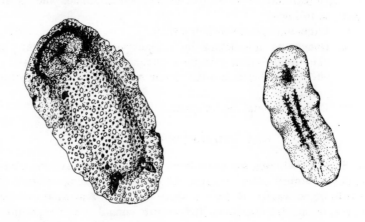

PLATE 6. Nudibranch and Flatworm.   "Wet Specimens."
  Any animal which has a high water content should be treated with replacement techniques and should not be dried. "Wet" specimens will shrink unless water is replaced by other material which will not evaporate from the cells.

EMBEDDING EQUIPMENT

5. The following list of equipment includes all of those things which are generally used during embedding processes:

    a. Molds of suitable size to fit the specimens.

    b. Graduated mixing cup. (Since American manufacturers use the English system of measurements in describing their formulas, the ordinary kitchen measuring cup calibrated in ounces is ideal. If metric measurements are used, the round figure of 30 cc per ounce is satisfactory for the converting of your figures from metric to English measurements.)

    c. Glass stirring rods,

    d. Shallow pan to be used as a water bath.

    e. Mold release. (Several brands are sold by various manufacturers of resin, such as Natcol, listed below. It has been found that a hard-drying paste wax, such as is used on hardwood floors, is also satisfactory.)

    f. Small forceps.

    g. Dull probes. (Orange sticks are satisfactory.)

    h. Embedding plastic with hardener and promoter. (Although various plastics were used in performing the experimentation for this book, most of the work was done with a NL 600 resin, obtainable from Natcol Products Company, P. O. Box 227, Redlands, California.

Catalysts should be used only with the intended brand.

The procedures described in this book eliminate the following equipment which might be indispensable when using other methods:

    a. Curing oven. (Some resins require continued high temperatures to bring about complete curing. NL 600 resin will cure satisfactorily in twenty-four hours at room temperature.)

    b. Power sanding equipment and polishing wheels. (The mold described in this book will produce a block with all six surfaces satisfactorily polished.)

MOLDS

6. Various containers have been used for moulding plastic mounts. Glass or ceramic containers are most widely used for this purpose. The Turtox Catalog, 1959, shows a picture of one of their laboratories where a worker is pouring a mount containing many specimens and using a large size pyrex baking dish. This

type of production would require sawing the block with a power saw, grinding the individual mounts and then polishing them on power equipment. This method of production is far too expensive and time consuming for use in a school or home laboratory.

Natcol, Plastic Embedding and Laminating, suggest many types of containers for moulding the liquid resin, including tin cans, paper cups, dishes, glass jars, boxes constructed of metal, wood or masonite and lined with cellophane, and even small paper boxes. All of the above are makeshift and do not solve the problem of grinding and polishing the finished mounts.   Ceramic molds are quite satisfactory, but are not available in a wide variety of sizes and shapes to fit the specimens.

7.   The mold described here and recommended by the author is especially designed to produce a plastic mount which has all six surfaces polished. It is of simple construction and is inexpensive. Construction details are shown on the accompanying plan.   Materials used in this construction are as follows:

   a. Strips of hardwood, birch or other fine-grained hardwood are preferred, 1/2" thick by 1 1/2" wide and in lengths which can be cut to desired lengths.

   b. Strips of the same hardwood 1/4" thick by 1 1/2" wide and in long lengths.

   c. Formica strips cut 1 1/2" wide and in lengths to fit the strips listed in a and b. The formica should be selected with the smoothest available surface and without texture.

   d. Contact cement recommended for binding formica (available at most hardware stores).

   e. Wood screws, size #6 and 3/4" long.   Round heads are preferred.

   f. Glass to be cut to fit the outside dimensions of the mold. (These pieces of glass form the mold bottoms.)

   g. Glass to be cut to fit the inside dimensions of the finished mold. (These are the cover-slips.)

   h. Cellophane tape 3/4" wide.

Following the directions given on the can of contact cement, face one side of each of the hardwood strips with formica. Measure the thickness of the 1/2" strip with formica attached and record this measurement for future use.

DETAIL CONSTRUCTION OF MOLD FOR CASTING RESIN MOUNTS FOR
EMBEDDING BIOLOGCAL SPECIMEN

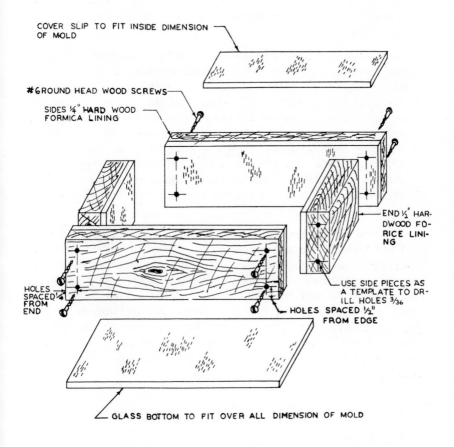

COVER SLIP TO FIT INSIDE DIMENSION
OF MOLD

#6ROUND HEAD WOOD SCREWS

SIDES ¼" HARD WOOD
FORMICA LINING

END ½" HAR-
DWOOD FO-
RICE LINI-
NG

USE SIDE PIECES AS
A TEMPLATE TO DR-
ILL HOLES 3/36

HOLES
SPACED ¼
FROM
END

HOLES SPACED ½"
FROM EDGE

GLASS BOTTOM TO FIT OVER ALL DIMENSION OF MOLD

PLATE 7.   Construction Drawing of Mold.

Decide upon the size of casting to be made.   As an example, a casting of the dimension of 1 1/2" by 2 1/2" is desired.   Cut two of the 1/2" strips to a length of 1 1/2" for the end pieces of the mold. Sand the ends of these two pieces until they are smooth and square. Cut two strips for the sides from the 1/4" faced wood. These should be 2 1/2" plus 2 times the thickness of the 1/2" faced pieces.   The thinner sides will overlap the end strips.

8.   Using a 3/32" drill, make two holes on each side of the pieces and centered at 1/4" from the end and 1/2" from the edge.   (A total of four holes per strip.)

Now assemble the sides against the end pieces with the formica lining inside the box and, using the existing holes just drilled as a guide, drill into the thicker piece.   As the pieces are lined up and drilled, mark them with identification numbers or letter so that the mold may be assembled in the same manner each time it is used. Change the size of the drill and ream the holes in the side pieces so that they will be oversized and a snug fit to the body of a #6 screw. Assemble the mold and draw all of the screws tight. If all of the pieces are not flush on the bottom edge, they should be sanded. This bottom edge must fit tight against the glass used as a bottom of the mold or leakage will occur.

Disassemble the mold and wax all of the formica surfaces. Clean and wax both sides of the bottom glass. Polish the waxed surfaces, reassemble and place the mold upside down on a table.   Place the bottom glass in position and strip all edges with 3/4" cellophane tape. Be sure that the tape adheres to both the wood and the glass.   The mold is now ready for use and it is time to proceed with the anchor layer.   Before pouring any plastic, however, you should try the cover glass and see that it slides easily and snugly into the mold. The illustration on the next page in Plate 8 shows various sizes of molds.

PLATE 8. <u>Photograph of various sizes and shapes of molds.</u>
It is advisable to construct several molds of various sizes and shapes. The molds may be cleaned and used over many times. They should be stored in a place that is free of both dust and moisture.

GENERAL EMBEDDING PROCEDURE

1. The general procedure for pouring the plastic is the same for all mounts whether wet or dry specimens are used. These are as follows:

a. Prepare the mold. Be sure that the corners and edges are tight and that all surfaces that will contact the liquid plastic have been waxed. (Some manufacturers prepare a special mold release for this purpose, but a good furniture wax has been found to be satisfactory.) All excess wax should be removed with a clean cloth.

b. Pour enough plastic into the measuring cup to make a base layer 1/8" thick in the bottom of all molds being prepared. Set the measuring cup in a hot water bath and bring the temperature of the water to boiling but do not boil. At this temperature the air bubbles will float to the surface of the plastic and the plastic itself will be quite liquid.

c. Remove the measuring cup from the water-bath and dry the outside with a cloth. It is very important that none of the condensed steam is allowed to drip into the plastic. Stir the plastic rapidly and in all directions while adding the proper amount of catalyst for "fast-setting" the formula. You may disregard air bubbles, since these give little or no trouble when using warm plastic.

d. Pour the plastic quickly into the various molds to a depth of 1/8". Set the measuring cup aside to be cleaned later and immediately inspect each mold for any bubbles of trapped air. These should be removed immediately by working them to the surface or to the edge of the mold with a probe. If mixing and pouring is done rapidly, very few bubbles will be found. Set the molds on a level surface and allow to stand until the base layer is set and not more than a slight tackiness remains.

e. At this point attention should be given to cleaning all glassware. Immerse all dirty equipment in a hot detergent solution and allow to soak for half an hour. (Tide, All, Oxydol, or any of the stronger household detergents may be used.) After soaking, wet a paper towel with the wash water and scrub all surfaces well. Rinse with hot, running water and dry with clean towels.

f. While waiting for the base layer to set, the specimens may be prepared for mounting. A number of techniques for the preparation of specimens are presented elsewhere in this book. When the specimen and base layer are ready, place the specimen on the tacky surface of the base layer and center it as desirable.

g. Prepare a second batch of plastic equal to that used for the base layer. This is to be the anchor layer and it should not cover the specimen entirely. If the specimen is small and a wet preparation, the same fast-setting formula may be used. If the specimen is large or if it has been dried, a slower setting formula is desirable. This allows more time for dispensing with any air bubbles that may arise. When all the bubbles have been dispersed, set the molds aside and proceed to clean all equipment.

h. The top layer may be mixed and poured as soon as the second layer (anchor layer) has gelled firmly. The time required for setting may vary considerably because of the temperature, light or other factors which affect the catalytic action. The gelling action may be checked by touching the specimen with a dull probe to see if it is held firmly in position. Enough plastic should be mixed this time to cover the specimen entirely and it is advisable to use the medium or slow-setting formula. For specimens under 1/4" thickness, the medium-setting formula is satisfactory. If more than 1/4" of plastic is to be poured, it is best to use the slow-setting formula.

Very large blocks should be poured in several layers of no more than 1/4" thickness per layer. The heat from the polymerization process is accumulative and, when in excess, may cause the block to crack.

Check for air bubbles as before and then proceed to clean all equipment.

i. The finishing layer may be poured when the block has become hard and only a slight tackiness remains on the surface. It will be noticed that polymerization starts at the bottom of each layer and proceeds toward the top. Mix enough fast-setting formula to cover the entire mount to a depth of 1/8". Pour this layer quickly and move the mold to cause the plastic to distribute itself quickly and evenly over the entire surface. Stand the cover-slip on edge in the soft plastic at one side of the mold and lower it into the plastic in such a manner that all of the air will be forced ahead of it to the far edge. Apply enough pressure to the center of the cover-slip to cause the plastic to ooze from around all four edges and form a puddle on top of the glass. Do not worry about the excess plastic.

It will be soft enough to be scraped away after the finishing layer has become firm underneath the glass.   If any trouble is encountered in removing all of the air from under the glass, it is likely that not enough plastic was used in the finishing layer.   The time saved in polishing this surface will more than pay for the plastic that is thrown away. (The above technique in placing the cover-slip is similar to that used when applying a cover-slip to a microscope slide.   If the cover-slip is lowered gently but firmly, no trouble should be encountered.)

Clean all equipment.

To summarize the above procedure:

1st layer .   .   .   . Base layer
2nd layer .   .   .   . Anchor layer
3rd layer .   .   .   . Top layer
4th layer .   .   .   . Finishing layer

2. Allow the mold to stand until the block is thoroughly set before attempting to remove it from the mold.   There is no rush at this point and all faces will have a better finish if a couple or three days are allowed for the final cure.

To remove the block from the mold, first remove all of the screws and take off the scotch tape which seals the bottom glass in place. Set the mold on a flat surface and insert the edge of a single-edge blade or scalpel edge into the joint where the formica of the end butts against the side of the mold.   Press the blade firmly into the crack and the side of the mold should separate and fall away. Occasionally it may be necessary to use slight pressure against the side piece in addition to the pressure of the blade. Repeat the same operation to remove the other side.   The end pieces may be removed by cutting along the edge of the cover-slip.   Next place the mount with both glasses attached in a bath of hot detergent water and allow to set for several minutes. This will usually separate both glasses, but, if not successful, the mount may be placed in a refrigerator and chilled.

When the plastic block is free from the glass all side faces should be perfectly smooth.   There will be a sharp, irregular edge around the entire block and this should be sanded away, using 250 grit emery cloth.   A good tool for this may be made by gluing the emery paper to both sides of a tongue depressor and using it as a file. Be careful to touch only the edges. Scratches on the highly finished surface are hard to remove.

The beginner is likely to pick up some of the soft plastic on his fingers and transfer it to the finished surfaces. If this should occur, the blotches may be removed by wiping with a soft cloth soaked in acetone.

PLATE 9. Removing the finished block from the mold.

3. Styrene Monomer is a light liquid sometimes referred to as plastic thinner. This liquid is compatible with NL-600 resin and may be used to an advantage with some specimens during the outlined procedure. In step (f) of the procedure a small amount of styrene monomer poured around and over the specimen will tend to rise to the top of the plastic as it is poured and will tend to float any fragile parts of the animal into the plastic at the same time. It will also aid in the escape of small air bubbles that may be trapped in folds or crevices. This procedure is elsewhere referred to as a "float layer". Do not worry about tackiness on the surface of the plastic when styrene monomer is used since it will disappear when the surface layer is poured.

PLATE 10.   A group of mounts as they were removed from the mold. No polishing is necessary.

Styrene monomer may also be used to thin raw plastic. A mixture of one part of styrene monomer to ten parts of the plastic has been used without apparent trouble. The mixture should be stirred thoroughly before adding the catalyst and the amount of catalyst should be determined by the original volume of plastic instead of the total volume of the mixture.

4. If you would prefer to use a different method than the coverslip for obtaining a polished surface, the following laminating procedure may be used. Clean and wax a piece of glass much larger than the surface of the mount to be laminated. (Double weight glass is most desirable for this.) Sand the surface to be finished until it is perfectly flat. This can be done easily by hand since only a roughly sanded surface is necessary. Mix a small amount of plastic with fast setting formula and pour a puddle in the center of the glass. Press the sanded surface of the block into this puddle and thus force the plastic to ooze from all edges. After two or three hours, scrape the excess plastic away from the block and wipe away the stickiness with a cloth soaked in acetone. Allow the block to set for another ten or twelve hours and then remove the glass by procedures described in paragraph #2 of this chapter.

COLLECTING, NARCOTIZATION
AND PREPARATION OF SPECIMENS

1. There is usually some danger of overcollecting in the field. When more specimens are taken than are needed they become a storage problem. A single good specimen of each species sought is sufficient unless specific studies are being made. When animals of a single species are abundant, carefully select one or two animals that are most representative of the species and are of a size which will be convenient to embed. Check your state laws and make sure that none of your specimens are protected. You may find that a collector's license is required. This may be obtained from the State Fish and Game Department. A collector's license may allow you to collect undersized specimens of the protected species within certain bag limits. This is an advantage if plastic mounts are to be prepared.

2. When planning a collecting trip, anticipate the type or even the species of animals that will be available. Most animals require special materials or equipment while in the field if they are to be killed and preserved to the best advantage. An example of this might be Tegula, the turban snail of the Pacific Coast tide pools. This animal will withdraw into its shell upon the least provocation, and will remain there with the operculum closed so tightly that preserving fluid cannot reach the soft body. The collector who would attempt to mount one of these uncured molluscs in plastic is doomed to meet with failure. Tegula, if treated properly, may be killed in an expanded condition so that the animal will cure and the body may be observed. Specimens have been prepared in expanded condition by keeping them alive in sea water and placing the jar containing them inside a refrigerator until thoroughly chilled. A bit of seaweed placed in the jar may also offer some encouragement. When expanded, place the jar in the refrigerator unit until small ice crystals form. The snail will become inactive at this temperature and may be transferred to another jar which contains cold AFA solution. Other molluscs, including limpets, will also react to this treatment. See page 26 for illustrations of properly expanded molluscs.

3. The basic equipment for collecting varies with the type of animal to be taken. The list of essentials should be made up ahead of time and excessive tools, containers, etc., should be avoided. It would be impossible to carry enough equipment at one time to

PLATE 11. Plastic Mounts of Marine Snail and Land Snail.
Many animals require narcotization before killing. Both of the
snails shown above would otherwise draw into their shells and close
the operculums.   The sea anemone (Plate 12) will draw into a tight
ball. The anemone and the marine snail (above left) are narcotized
with magnesium chloride. The land snail (above right) is treated
with chloriform vapor in a closed jar.

handle the problems encountered in collecting all types of animals.
It is best to restrict the collecting list and make a sincere effort to
do the job well with proper observations and notes. A small pocket
notebook and pencil should accompany the serious student at all
times.

4. Many procedures may be found for relaxing specific animals
before killing. A well relaxed animal always makes a better specimen. In addition to the narcotization by chilling mentioned in paragraph #2, warm water is sometimes equally as good. This is best
accomplished by pouring small amounts of warm water into the

habitat water over a long period of time. Killing should not be attempted until the animal no longer withdraws from being touched
with a probe. Drugs are sometimes used to relax animals. Some
of the recommended drugs are listed below:

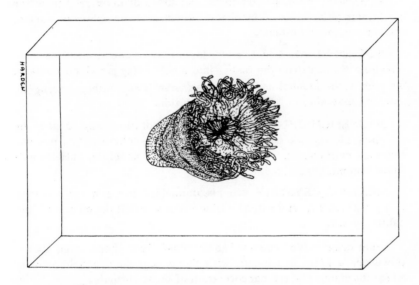

PLATE 12. <u>Plastic Mount of Sea Anemone,</u> showing animal relaxed after narcotization with magnesium chloride.

CHLORAL HYDRATE, 2% solution may be added drop by drop to
the habitat water of planaria, flukes, nemerteans, barnacles and
leeches. After a few minutes note the expanded parts and check
narcotization by touching them with a probe. If the animal does not
react, it may be transferred immediately to the fixing solution.

CARBONATED WATER. Unflavored soda water is recommended
for sea anemones. It should be added slowly to the habitat water
and narcotization can be checked as suggested above.

CHLOROFORM or ETHER are used for killing most vertebrates
and land snails. Reptiles may be handled more easily if placed in
refrigeration until they reach a state of temporary hibernation and
then anaesthetized. Killing may be hastened by injecting a few milliliters of 50% alcohol into the abdominal cavity through the vent.
(See plate 22.)

CLOVE OIL placed on the surface of the habitat water containing small crustaceans, such as copepods, pill bugs, etc. , will render them inactive without causing panic, which so often causes the loss of legs.

ETHANOL, when in 70% form and added drop by drop to water containing polychaete, oligochaete, sipunculoid or echuroid worms, narcotizes these animals.

ISOPROPYL ALCOHOL in 70% form may be used for killing most insects. Simply drop the insect into a collecting jar which contains an inch of the alcohol and it will die instantly and without a struggle. Spiders may also be killed in this solution.

MAGNESIUM CHLORIDE in saturated solution may be used by dropping slowly into habitat water containing echinoderms, coelenterates, molluscs, protochordates and some annelids, until the animals become narcotized.

MENTHOL CRYSTALS are recommended for general use with many marine invertebrates. Place a few crystals on top of the habitat water.

Other drugs have been used as successfully as those listed above. However, a little experience with those suggested should provide adequate means for the narcotization of most animals.

SOME SPECIAL TECHNIQUES FOR
MOUNTING AND PRESERVING

1. Beetles and other insects with hard chitinous coverings are sometimes difficult to mount in plastic. The chitinous material does not seem to bond well with the plastic and a silvering effect is liable to occur. In spite of this it is worthwhile to try various specimens since the advantages of the mounts completed will outweigh an occasional loss. Since the animals will be exposed to liquid treatment throughout the embedding process, the killing technique mentioned in the previous chapter is most satisfactory. Wings of butterflies and moths will become transparent, but few scales are lost and the color will be retained. Appendages will become firmly set in the alcohol and will not break easily if the animal is dried during the mounting process. Insects which require no mounting may be transferred to 100% ethylene glycol for six or eight hours, drained for a few minutes on absorbent paper and then mounted directly in the plastic. Various stages in the life history of insects may be accumulated over a period of time and kept in the alcohol until the set is complete and ready to mount.

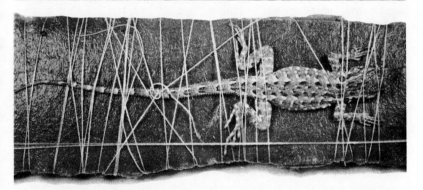

PLATE 13. <u>Photograph of lizard mounted for cure.</u> All vertebrates and many of the larger invertebrates should be mounted and tied in position before placing in the preservative. Unless this is done the hardened tissues will result in a distorted pose. The octopus on the book's cover was also mounted in a similar manner.

2. Large, cold-blooded vertebrates, including amphibians, reptiles and fish, require special handling. A small incision is made

in the ventral surface and all of the internal organs are removed.
Pack the cavity with cotton soaked with 10% formalin.   In most
instances it is best to flush the cavity well before packing.   Place
the animal on a piece of cardboard and arrange the legs, tail and
head in a lifelike position.   Wrap cloth or string around the cardboard and the animal to hold it in the desired pose during the curing period.   (See Plate 13.)   It may be necessary to weigh the
animal down with strips of lead when it is placed in the preserving
tray.   C. M. E. F3 preservative has been found excellent for these
animals (see page 37).

3.   In addition to the treatment above, fish should have small
blocks of cardboard cut to support the fins.   These may be held in
place with insect pins.   Ordinary pins will rust and leave stains on
the animal.   Another means of fastening the supports in place is to
use a needle and thread.

4.   The seashore offers one of the finest collecting grounds.
Every phylum of animal life is represented there and such a great
variety makes it impossible to use a single, simple technique that
will fit all cases.   For this reason it is best to transport the loot
alive and in fresh sea water.   If it is impossible to transport live
specimens, refer to paragraph 8 in next chapter for the proper
preservative.   Be sure that any formalin used is free from acid.
Many marine animals have calciferous parts which can be damaged
by acid.

5.   Mammals and birds (when allowed by law) may be trapped by
using a box trap or some other device which causes no injury.   It
is best to kill them by careful use of chloroform in a closed box,
and then the insides taken out through a small abdominal incision.
Be sure to puncture the diaphragm and remove the lungs and heart.
Wash the body cavities well with formalin solution and then mount
the animal on cardboard, using a wide gauze bandage to hold it in
position.   Straighten all hair or feathers before applying the bandage.   Few mammals are small enough to mount well in plastic, but
embryonic forms are very adaptable.   Birds' wings, beaks and tal-
ons may be mounted for comparative studies.

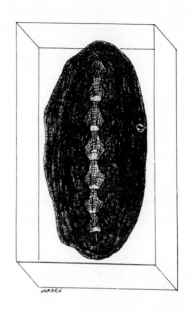

PLATE 14. <u>Starfish and Chitons in Plastic Mounts.</u> Some of the smaller specimens will present a better appearance if tied with a string or cloth to a piece of cardboard before preserving, as des-

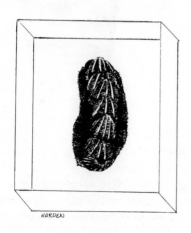

cribed in paragraph #2. The two animals on the left were cured without mounting. Notice the distorted arm on the starfish (upper left) and the tense curvature of the chiton (lower left), as compared with the relaxed appearance of the mounted and tied chiton (shown in the upper right).

PLATE 15. Marine Specimens.   Many fine specimens may be picked up along the beach or captured alive at low tide. The empty shells, such as the marine snail (upper left), may be mounted without curing, as can dried hydroids, like the ostrich-plume hydroid (lower left). The volcano limpet (upper right) and sand pillbug (on lower right) were collected alive and required curing and dehydration.

FIXING SOLUTIONS

1. Immediately after death cells begin to deteriorate. Complex molecules, which are relatively stable in living protoplasm, break down under the digestive action of bacteria and fungi. These invading organisms, which battle for existence in living tissue, no longer meet the resistance they once found and reproduce rapidly. The smaller molecules that result from this bacterial digestion change the internal osmitic pressure of cells and some shrinkage occurs. If the tissue of an animal is to be well preserved, it must be fixed immediately after death. The fixing solution should counteract as many of these changes as possible and the cell parts should remain firm so that they retain their size and shape.

2. There is no single chemical that could be termed a perfect fixative. Ten percent neutral formalin is most universally used as a single reagent; however, it does allow some shrinkage. Also, since formalin is a reducing agent, it sometimes acts upon organic pigments, causing them to fade. Acetic acid tends to bring about turgidity and reacts with calcium carbonate in bone or other animal parts. Alcohol is not a good fixative by itself since some bacteria survive in weak alcohol solutions. Stronger alcohols produce a dehydrating effect causing freshly killed animals to shrivel even though the same dehydration may be effective on tissue which is fixed in other solutions.

3. Chemical mixtures are most often used by micrologists. These mixtures have been standardized and are quite specific in their uses. Some of the mixtures contain metallic salts, which penetrate cell parts and may be used later as mordants for stains. Some solutions are recommended because of their ability to penetrate and preserve specific cell parts, such as mitochondria or nuclei. These qualities have little value unless microscopic sections are to be prepared. Other formulae are designed for specific types of tissue. In this book the major interest will be in preserving whole specimens, but much general information can be gained by studying general micrological techniques.

4. Fixing solutions should be mixed accurately. Variation in the concentration of a solution may change its properties entirely. Since many good formulae have been published for mixing small quantities of solution (up to 250 milligrams), many of these formulae must be converted for use where larger quantities are required.

The metric system is most often used and, since one milliliter of water weighs one gram at zero degrees Centigrade, the percentage of solution by weight or volume is considered as interchangeable. A method of dilution often used by micrologists in the adjustment of liquid concentrations is as follows:

The liquid to be diluted is measured in milliliters in an amount equal to the desired concentration and then diluted with distilled water to an amount, in milliliters, equal to the original concentration of the reagent.

Example: To dilute 95% ethyl alcohol to 40% concentration, measure 40 milliliters of alcohol and add distilled water to bring the entire volume of the mixture to 95 milliliters. When gross amounts of a reagent are needed, this method may be converted to the following formula:

$$V_2 = \frac{V_1 \ C_1}{C_2}$$

or . . .

$$V_1 = \frac{C_2 \ V_2}{C_1}$$

C_1 is the concentration of the original reagent.

C_2 is the concentration desired.

V_1 is the volume of the original reagent.

V_2 is the final volume of the mixed solution.

Example: How much 95% alcohol will be needed to mix one liter of 70% alcohol solution?

C_1 = 95

C_2 = 70

V_2 = 1000 milliliters

substituting . . . $V_1 = \frac{70 \ \times \ 1000}{95}$ = 716 ml.

Thus, 716 milliliters of 95% alcohol diluted to one liter will make a 70% solution.

5. The same formula may be applied when using a solid reagent, which is to be mixed to a specific concentration. In this case V_1 would be expressed in grams and C_1 would be expressed as 100%.

Example: How much sodium hydroxide is required to mix one liter of 2% solution?

$$V_1 = \frac{2 \times 1000}{100} = 20 \text{ grams.}$$

Thus, 20 grams of sodium hydroxide dissolved in water and diluted to one liter will be a 2% solution.

6. Some standard reagents and their concentration as usually sold by suppliers are given below:

Ethyl Alcohol (Pure C. P.)	95%
Isopropyl Alcohol (rubbing compound)	70%
Formalin (standard reagent)	40%
Phenol (C. P. or pure liquid)	90%
Hydrogen Peroxide	03%

When purchasing reagents be sure that the concentration is printed on the label or is listed in the catalog.

7. Absolute or 100% alcohol may be prepared from 95% alcohol by adding powdered, anhydrous copper sulfate to the alcohol and keeping it tightly corked. Shake the mixture and allow to stand for several hours. The copper sulfate will take up the water from the alcohol and turn blue. Decant the alcohol into a clean, dry bottle and repeat the operation several times until the copper sulfate fails to show the blue color due to water absorption. At this time some workers prefer to filter the alcohol and store it in a clean, dry and tightly-corked bottle. It is just as well, however, to leave the copper sulfate in the bottle as an indicator. If there is any leakage of air so that the alcohol absorbs slight traces of water, it will be removed by the copper sulfate. Since copper sulfate settles to the bottom, it is easy to decant off small amounts of pure, absolute alcohol as needed.

8. Ten percent formalin is used most often as a curing agent. It may be prepared by diluting 250 milliliters of commercial formalin to one liter with distilled water.

A handy method of preparing 10% formalin in the field is as follows: Carry several 250 milliliter amounts of formalin in small bottles in the collecting kit. Measure liter amounts of water and mark the graduations with paint or tape on the sides of the collecting pail. When collecting, use the habitat water of the animals to dilute the formalin by using a single 250 milliliter bottle for each liter of solution.

A still better preservative can be prepared from sea water by using one 250 milliliter bottle of formalin and one 250 milliliter bottle of glyoxal for each liter of sea water solution. Most marine invertebrates will cure in this solution and require no further care in the laboratory.

9. A solution of 30% isopropyl alcohol is satisfactory for temporarily fixing animals in the field, but the animals should be changed to a formalin preservative upon arrival in the laboratory. Isopropyl alcohol may be purchased from most markets or drug stores as a rubbing compound. As a temporary preparation this compound may be diluted with an equal amount of water. Some bacteria will thrive in this solution so it is not considered as a laboratory reagent. If it is necessary to leave a specimen in this solution for more than a day or two, the solution should be drained off and changed to a fresh mixture. If the alcohol preservative becomes milky or cloudy, it is an indication that spoilage has occurred. A little practice will develop a sensitiveness to the slight odor given off by decay in alcohol so the solution may be changed before milkiness occurs.

10. A F A solution is highly recommended for killing most worms as well as all other types of invertebrates which need to be killed quickly and kept in expanded condition. This solution not only kills quickly but hardens the tissue so that little shrinkage will occur in subsequent curing solutions. Animals should not be left in this solution for more than an hour since the acid will attack calceriferous structures and since many pigments will either change color or bleach entirely if left indefinitely.

The solution may be mixed as follows:
<pre>
    70% ethyl alcohol . .   .   .   440 milliliters
    Commercial formalin   .   .   .   .   .   50 milliliters
    Glacial Acetic Acid .   .   .   .   .   .   10 milliliters
</pre>

Use the above solution full strength. Do not dilute.

11. C.M.E. F3, developed by Mr. Lutz for Natcol Laboratories, is a very effective fixative. It has an advantage over some of the other fixatives since it can be used universally and since animals may be left in the solution for an indefinite curing time without further attention. It may be prepared as follows:

Commercial formalin . . . . . . 30 milliliters
Glyoxal (30%) . . . . . . 30 milliliters
Sodium chloride . . . . . . 200 grams
Sodium sulfite . . . . . . 5 grams
Distilled water to mix one liter

Animals should not be moved out of this solution too soon. The high salt content maintains an osmotic equilibrium and little if any shrinkage occurs. Animals will also be found to be more flexible and fragile parts do not break so easily.

It will be noted that the preservative mentioned in paragraph #8 as mixed from sea water in the field is almost identical to the above.

12. Gilson's Fluid, an old standard with the micrologists, is highly recommended for killing and preserving small worms and larva. It penetrates quickly and does not shrink the tissue. It may be prepared as follows:

Solution 1 . . . . Dissolve 10 grams of mercuric chloride in 100 milliliters of distilled water and add 1 milliliter of concentrated nitric acid.

Solution 2 . . . . Mix separately one gram of chromic acid in 100 milliliters of distilled water and add 1 milliliter glacial acetic acid.

Combine the two solutions. This will make slightly more than 200 milliliters of solution.

Since Gilson's Fluid is highly acid it will destroy calcium carbonate.

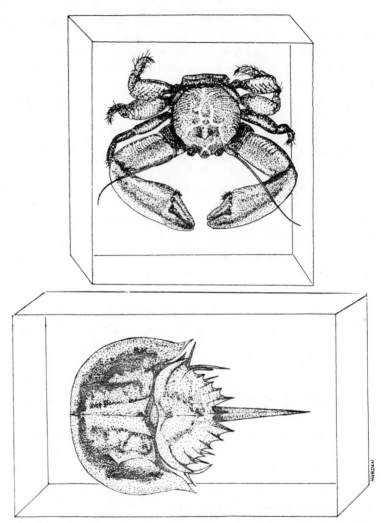

PLATE 16. Porcelain Crab (above) and Horseshoe Crab (below).
The two crabs above are both good examples of variation in pigments, which offer a challenge to those interested in color preservation.   The porcelain crab will turn a bright red if hydrocarbon
derivatives of single bond series are used.   This color· change is
most noted in alcohol or acetone. Both specimens seem to cure best
in C. M. E. F-3 (see page 37), and may then be dried by the silica-
gel method (see page 39) or in warm air. They should be soaked a
few minutes in styrene monomer before placing in the plastic. The
horseshoe crab may be cured in 10% formalin.

DEHYDRATION

1. Since polyester embedding resins are incompatible with water and since all curing solutions are aqueous, it is necessary to use a dehydrating agent. Some specimens may be dried in air, but shrinkage will occur in most cases. Air drying has been successful with crabs and other arthropods, which have heavy exoskeletons. Most appendages become very brittle on these animals and extreme care must be used to keep them intact. When air drying is used, the animals should be placed in liquid resin to which a drop of catalyst has been added and allowed to stand until the resin has replaced all of the air. Otherwise air bubbles will be given off later during the hardening process.

Liquid dehydration is more effective and eliminates the trouble with air bubbles. In general, liquid dehydration is accomplished by soaking the specimen in a liquid which absorbs the water and gradually replaces it with a compatible chemical that will not interfere with the polymerization action of the plastic. This is brought about by a slow process of water molecules moving out of the cells and being replaced by other molecules. Dilution of the dehydrating agent results and several changes of this solution may be required to complete the process.

Some effective dehydrants are listed below.

2. Ethylene Glycol is compatible with most resins and may be used in commercial concentrations without dilution. If the water content in the specimen is high, it might be most advisable to use an 80% solution of alcohol first and then transfer to the glycol. Mr. Lutz also suggests the use of propylene glycol for the same purpose. The dehydrating time for small specimens is twenty-four to forty-eight hours. When changing the specimen to a fresh solution, allow it to drain for a few minutes on a clean absorbent paper. Specimens treated with glycol may be transferred directly to plastic after a blotting with absorbent tissue.

3. Silica gel is often used with the glycols for removing the last trace of water. Upon removing the specimen from the glycol, wrap it in absorbent paper tissue and place it in a desiccator (oven or other means of drying) on top of a layer of dehydrated silica gel. If an oven is used, the temperature should be kept low (under 140 degrees). Cover with other layers of absorbent tissue and add another layer of silica gel to the surface. After forty-eight hours in the desiccator the specimen should be ready to embed.

HARDEN

PLATE 17. <u>Butterfly.</u> Winged insects, such as butterflies, wasps, dragonflies and others, may be mounted on flat insect mounting boards and dried in air. They may be removed from the mounting board and dipped in styrene monomer, then placed directly in freshly poured plastic. This will eliminate many of the problems with air bubbles.

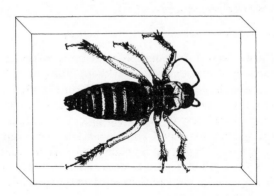

PLATE 18. <u>Jerusalem Cricket.</u> Grasshoppers, crickets and other heavy-bodied insects should be cured by dropping into ethylene glycol. They should be blotted on paper tissues and then placed in a desiccator with silica gel for dehydration. A short soaking time in styrene monomer before mounting will help to eliminate problems with air bubbles.

Silica gel may be dehydrated for re-use by placing it in an oven at 400 degrees F. A small amount of cobalt salts added to the silica gel will act as an indicator to tell when all of the water has been removed. If water is present, the cobalt salts will become a light pink color and can hardly be told from pieces of the silica gel itself, but, when dehydration is complete, the salts will become deep blue and will remain so as long as the gel is useful. By reclaiming the silica gel after each use, it will last indefinitely.

In using this method of dehydration the specimens will appear somewhat moist when fully dehydrated since much of the glycol will be retained by them. This has no effect whatever on the embedding process.

4. Ethyl alcohol has been used with some specimens as a dehydrator. This is the standard histological or micrological technique of using progressively stronger concentrations of alcohol solution, starting with a 40% solution and increasing the concentration of each successive step by 10%. Final dehydration requires absolute grade (100%) alcohol (see page 35). Ethyl alcohol or ethyl ether will reduce the haemoglobin in blood-filled tissue to iron, which results in a yellowish-brown color. For this reason ether is not recommended and alcohol should be used only where the deep brown color will add to the usefulness of the specimen. (See paragraph #3 in next chapter.) Isopropyl alcohol, 95% grade, is a good dehydrating agent and does not produce the extreme color change of ethyl alcohol. The specimen should be run through several changes of this reagent and then washed through acetone before embedding. After dipping in acetone, place the specimen on absorbent paper tissue and allow to drain for ten minutes before embedding.

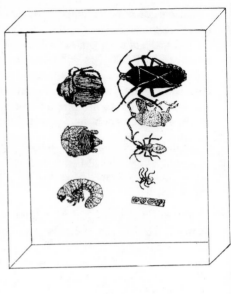

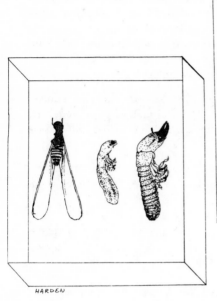

HARDEN

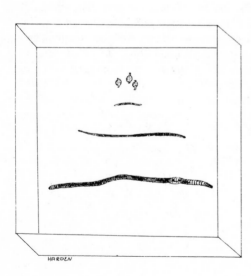

HARDEN

PLATE 19. Complica-
ted Museum Mounts.

An imaginative mind is
able to create a number
of useful and interesting
mounts such as:

Types of termites (on
left above).

Comparison of com-
plete and incomplete
metamorphosis. (Above
on right.)

Earthworm life history
(lower left).

PIGMENTS AND THEIR PRESERVATION

1. Natural pigments are difficult to preserve. Many of the original organic dyes found in animals are affected by changes in pH concentration. * Some pigments are easily oxidized or reduced and still others are soluble in chemicals that are used in preserving, dehydrating or mounting. No effective method of preservation of color will apply to all pigments. However, Mr. Lutz suggests that sodium sulfite and thiourea are effective in the preservation of some colors. These salts may be added to preserving solutions in a proportion of 1 gram of thiourea and .75 gram of sodium sulfite to each 100 milliliters of the solution treated.

A general consideration for all of those who become involved with pigments and color problems is the pH of the preserving and fixing solutions. Formalin, when used, will oxidize to form formic acid. Edwards found that "when the color of a preparation has deteriorated . . . . . the pH of the fluid needs readjusting." A good selective indicator paper may be used to check the pH, which should be maintained between 7.4 and 7.8. It is best to use fresh, neutral formalin when possible, but if acid formalin is used, the pH may be adjusted by the addition of small amounts of sodium carbonate.

The carotenoid pigments offer one of the largest problems in color preservation. In living tissue these substances are held in association with the protein molecules and as soon as death upsets this delicate balance the pigments fade and change in color. Heating or drying in any sense may bring about extreme changes. Although many people are working on the mystery that surrounds these pigments, it may be some time before a method of preservation in their original state is found and until then we can expect no more than an anatomical likeness of the true animal. It is a good idea to supplement mounts of such specimens with a color photograph or colored painting so that the student who inspects the mounted specimen will not be misled.

*pH is a chemical symbol that is used in indicating the amount of acidity or alkalinity in any given material or chemical mixture. It ranges from pH 0 (high acidity) to pH 14 (high alkalinity). 7 is even.

VARIETY IN PREPARATION

1. There are two main classifications of mounts that might be prepared for zoological study.

First, the general anatomical mount that is designed to show the external characteristics of an animal.

Second, the specific anatomical mount which points up certain specific systems, organs, or structures.

Within the first category might be ecological studies of groups of animals, developmental studies, such as metamorphic cycles of insects, commensal animals and single specimens. The second category might include cleared and stained preparations, dissections or injections. A single animal might suggest an entire series of mounts that might be used for demonstration in teaching various student groups.

Example -- <u>Rana</u> <u>pipiens</u> (grass frog):

Mount a . . . External characteristics. Mount the animal in a sitting or jumping position and preserve the natural coloration of the skin.

Mount b . . . Life history, including egg mass, tadpole, tadpole with hind legs, tadpole with front legs, tadpole with tail almost completely absorbed, and young frog.

Mount c . . . Adult frog stained and cleared to show the skeletal structure.

Mount d . . . Adult frog cleared and with both the skeleton and cartilage stained.

Mount e . . . Adult frog cleared and with the nervous system stained.

Mount f . . . Ventral dissection showing the visceral cavity and organs.

Mount g . . . Ventrally dissected frog with doubly injected circulatory system and cleared of other organs to facilitate better viewing.

No doubt there are many other possibilities, but it will be noted that each mount describes a specific study use. Likewise, each mount would require a specific method of preparation.

If the same set of mounts were to be planned, using a perch as the specimen, different problems would face the operator. The differences in cellular chemistry between different groups of animals may require adjustments in the time that is required or the concentrations of agents used in processing.

A few tested methods might be considered as standards to guide the beginner since they will usually produce acceptable results. We will consider them as general techniques.

In a very broad sense all animals might be grouped into two divisions for the purpose of selecting the proper technique for embedding:

      a. Animals which have soft unprotected bodies and which will shrink upon drying.

      b. Animals with exoskeletons or hard dermal structures which support the outer surface and which will withstand some degree of drying without shrinkage.

The latter group of animals are much more easily dealt with and you may find either the air drying or silica gel drying method described on page 39 as suitable.

The former group of animals are most successfully embedded when "wet techniques" are used throughout the process. The technique most adaptable to specific animals can only be determined by experimentation. Among the wet techniques listed, specific recommendations have been tested and found suitable for recommended animals.

2. General Technique I.

This treatment will partially clear the animal and give it a slight brownish or amber color. It has been used for embedding a pig fetus and it is possible to observe general internal details of the animal. Viewing this mount reminds one of examining the animal by x-ray or fluoroscope. Most young mammals and some of the other vertebrates should react to this treatment. If there is hair or if heavy skin pigments are present, the animal should be carefully skinned first.

Step A . . . Cure the animal in 10% formalin. Be sure to inject formalin into the visceral cavity and the cranium. Do not rush the curing time. Several weeks must be allowed for even a small specimen.

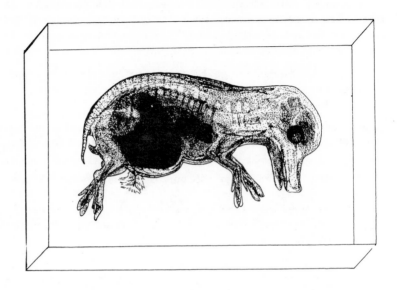

PLATE 20. <u>Pig Fetus in Mount.</u>

Step B . . . Remove the animal from the curing solution and transfer it to 50% isopropyl alcohol for twenty-four hours. Remove to 70% isopropyl alcohol for twenty-four hours and then make a final transfer to 95% alcohol for twelve hours.

Step C . . . Transfer the specimen from the 95% alcohol to acetone for four to six hours. If the acetone becomes cloudy, it should be changed to a fresh solution. The used acetone may be saved and used as a first step for other specimens, but should be discarded when the milky appearance becomes dominant.

Step D . . . Remove the specimen from the acetone and allow it to stand in air until most of the acetone has evaporated. Fifteen minutes is usually sufficient for this.

Step E . . . Place the specimen in styrene monomer. If the dehydrating process was carried out well, the tissues should be transparent within six hours.

Step F . . . Prepare a bath of plastic by adding one drop of catalyst to each ounce of plastic. Place the animal in this bath for several hours to allow for complete penetration. This may be observed from time to time and the quality of transparency will improve as penetration takes place. As soon as the penetration is complete, the animal is ready for mounting by the procedure described in paragraph #6 of Chapter 1.

3. General Technique II.

This is a variation of Technique I and was used with flukes that were cleared and stained with eosin. Ethyl alcohol was substituted for the isopropyl alcohol for dehydration. Dehydration was started in 50% solution and the concentration was increased by 10% steps to absolute grade. One hour was required for each step. Staining was done by adding a few drops of eosin to the 50% solution. (The method of dip staining in eosin may be applied at this point. Other than for the staining, the procedure will be the same as for the General Technique I.)

4. General Technique III.

This is the technique that is usually employed when external characteristics are to be retained. Specimens prepared in this manner should be mounted as described in paragraph #2 in Chapter 2.

Step A . . . Specimens mounted for external examination may be cured in C. M. E. F-3. Do not rush the curing time and inject body cavities well with a hypodermic syringe. A month or six weeks curing time is recommended for a complete cure.

Step B . . . Drain the specimen for half an hour on a paper towel or other absorbent material; then place in a bath of 33% ethylene glycol. Allow to stand for forty-eight hours; then drain and transfer to 70% glycol for the same amount of time. Drain the specimen upon removal from this solution and inject all body cavities, including the brain case, with full strength ethylene glycol. Before injection of any body cavity, it is a good procedure to use the hypodermic syringe for removal of all possible liquid from the cavity. Now, place the injected specimen in full strength ethylene glycol and allow to stand for at least twenty-four hours.

Step C . . . Remove the specimen onto paper towels and allow to drain for half an hour. Wipe away all excess glycol, using absorbent tissue. Place the animal in the mold and proceed with the embedding. Pour the first layer (anchor layer) so that it drains over and around every part of the specimen. This will keep the tissue from drying excessively until the next layer is poured.

5. General Technique IV. (For insects and spiders.)

Kill the animal in isopropyl alcohol and allow to stand in this solution for two or three days. Transfer to full strength ethylene glycol for twenty-four hours; then drain and mount. For butterflies and other insects, which are mounted with wings expanded, use a mounting board as pictured in Plate 17. Notice that the mounting board is flat or nearly so and differs in this way from the usual insect mounting board that slopes up on either side at an angle. Allow the spread specimen to dry thoroughly for at least five days before placing in plastic. The specimen should be placed in the mold with the ventral side up and enough styrene monomer dropped over the animal to wet the wings and body well.

6. General Technique V.

This procedure is used on many types of specimens. It is found to be best for small crustacea.

Steps A and B . . . Follow the general procedure used in Technique III.

Step C . . . Remove the specimen from the glycol and wrap in absorbent tissue. Soak the tissue in fresh ethylene glycol and place in a desiccator with silica gel. Leave undisturbed in the desiccator for 48 hours (at no higher temperature than 140 degrees).

Step D . . . Place the specimen in the mold and add enough styrene monomer to cover the base layer about 1/16" deep. Pour the plastic in the usual manner.

7. General Technique VI.

The following technique was used by David Harden in preparing a complete descriptive study of Acmaeidae of the Pacific Coast of North America. The animal and its shell were mounted separately and together in the same mount. The body parts of the animal became clear, but the natural color was maintained. The same technique was successful, using a clam as a specimen. These mounts might be considered to be of some anatomical value.

Step A . . . Cure for several days in 10% formalin.

Step B . . . Dehydrate through three stages of isopropyl

alcohol; 50%, 70% and 95%.

Step C . . . Carefully removed the animal from its shell by probing with a small scalpel along the mantle. From this point the animal and its corresponding shell must be kept together and in separate vials.

Step D . . . Remove the animal to xylol and allow to stand until partially cleared. The time may vary from thirty minutes to as much as two hours. This is possibly due to a variation of the penetration of the alcohol.

Step E . . . Remove to styrene monomer for two hours and then embed by the usual procedure.

8. General Technique VII.

The glycerine method has been used rather extensively in the past so we shall repeat it here. It may be used for soft-bodied invertebrates as well as insects or spiders.

Dilute glycerine with the base solution used for preserving. If alcohol was used in the curing, dilute with 70% alcohol. If formaldehyde was used, dilute with distilled water. In this manner prepare glycerine solutions of the following concentrations: 10%, 25%, 50% and 75%.

Soak the specimen in the 10% solution for 24 hours; then run through each of the other concentrations successively to the 100% glycerine. Allow a soaking period of twenty-four hours for each step. Transfer the specimen from the 100% glycerine to absolute alcohol and allow to stand until there is no further evidence that glycerine is still coming from the specimen. This can be determined by watching for the clear lines which flow away from the specimen. Next dry the specimen in air and then transfer to uncatalyzed plastic. Make several changes in the plastic, allowing the specimen to soak for several hours in each change. The plastic will become cloudy as the remaining glycerine continues to emerge from the surface.

Mount as usual.

This procedure is usually more time consuming and expensive than other procedures outlined earlier and could possibly be considered as obsolete, but may be worth experimenting with.

Many special techniques are used by micrologists and are adaptable to plastic mounting. A little skill and practice is needed to obtain the best results and some modifications of the original technique might be necessary to meet specifications of the plastic. Two of these by Thurlow C. Nelson have been modified and used with some success. Lipman (Stain Technology, X. 1935, 61) writes: "Skeletons fixed in alchol and cleared in KOH will stain selectively with Alazarin Red S (1 part of Alazarin to 10,000 parts of 2% solution of KOH)."

The other suggested technique involves selective staining of nerves in cleared whole animals. (By "cleared" is meant that all viscera that interfere with seeing the nervous system have been cleared away.)

Another useful staining method that has given good results with flukes and small hydroids and hydroid medusa is a dip staining method, using eosin in alcohol.

All of these techniques will be described in more detail.

CLEARING ANIMALS IN KOH

9. Potassium Hydroxide (KOH) has been used in clearing the bodies of vertebrates so that stained bone, cartilage and nerve tissue may be clearly seen. Various strengths of KOH solution have been used from as high as 5% to as low as 1%. Weaker solutions tend to clear slowly, but are easier to control. The following procedure seemed to give good results. The animal was killed in 70% alcohol (either ethyl or isopropyl may be used). Remove the animal from the alcohol before the joints become stiff and mount in an extended manner so that the internal anatomy will be positioned properly.

The same mounting methods may be used as described in paragraph #2 on page 29. Wash the visceral cavity with water and bleach for one hour in .03% hydrogen peroxide. Place in KOH (1% solution is recommended) and immerse with lead weights until all the tissue is clear and the bone is visible. The clearing may take from one to three days, depending on the size of the animal. If clearing seems too slow, remove the animal by drawing off the solution with a bulb syringe and replace with fresh solution. The animal itself will become very soft and should not be disturbed more than necessary. The jelly-like tissues will be hardened in a later step and there is no need to worry about the appearance of the tissue at this stage.

STAINING THE SKELETON

10. When all of the skeletal structure is clearly visible in the translucent, jelly-like body, change to a fresh solution of 1% KOH and add a solution of Alizarin Red S, drop by drop, until the entire solution is a deep, purplish-red color. After twenty-four hours change to a fresh solution and add fresh dye. This may be repeated several times, depending upon the penetration of the dye. When the bone is visibly a deep cherry-red color, destain the other tissues by changing to a 70% isopropyl alcohol solution to which 1% hydrochloric acid is added drop by drop.

ALIZARIN RED S

11. Alizarin Red S is a soluble acid dye used to stain calcified bone cells.

Synonyms: Alizarin Red (water soluble), Alizarin Carmine.

Preparation: Dissolve 1 gram Alizarin Red S in 100 milliliters of distilled water. This concentration may be stored in a dropper cap bottle for an indefinite time. Solubility in water at 26 degrees C is 7.69%, in alcohol at 26 degrees C is .15%. (Conn, Biological Stains, 6th Edition, 1953.)

PREPARATIONS OF STAINED ANIMALS FOR MOUNTING

12. Replace the destaining solution with fresh 70% alcohol for one hour. At this time change to 80% alcohol for another hour; then replace with 95% alcohol. At the end of thirty minutes transfer to acetone for half an hour and then place the specimen in styrene monomer overnight. Mix a batch of thinned plastic (mounting plastic one part and one part of styrene monomer to which one drop of hardener has been added for each ounce) and immerse the animal in this for several minutes or until the tissues are quite transparent. If air bubbles appear inside of the animal, some of the thinned plastic may be worked into the tissue to replace the air, or cavities may be injected with a hypodermic needle. When the acetone has been replaced by plastic, the animal is ready for mounting. Use a float layer of styrene monomer with the procedure described in paragraph #3, page 23.

CARTILAGE STAINING

12. Cartilage staining is described by Earnest L. Lutz. This technique may be combined with the above procedure to give double-stained mounts with blue cartilage and red bone.

Procedure: As soon as the animal is killed and prepared for clearing, immerse it in a solution of Toluidine Blue. (Toluidine Blue, mixed in 1 gram, as 400 milliliters of 70% isopropyl alcohol, and 4 milliliters of 6N hydrochloric acid.) It will take from 3 to 10 days for penetration, depending on the size of the animal. Submerge the animal and change the solution each day. Destain in acid-alcohol solution (4 milliliters, 6N HCL, 400 milliliters of isopropyl alcohol), changing daily until a slight tint of the dye is seen in the solution. Clear the animal as described in paragraph #9, page 50, and continue by staining the bone with Alizarin Red S.

STAINING NERVES

14. Thurlow C. Nelson's technique for staining nerve tissues is described in <u>Animal</u> <u>Micrology</u> by Guyer. This technique offers possibilities for plastic embedding. Some variation of the technique might have to be made for successful application.

DIP STAINING IN EOSIN

15. Cleared and stained flukes and <u>Aurelia</u> (a jellyfish) have been prepared in the following manner:

After preserving in 10% formalin the animal was dehydrated in ethyl alcohol, starting with a 50% solution and progressing through 10% steps to a 70% solution. One hour is required for each step. Have a solution of eosin prepared (1 gram of eosin in 50 milliliters of 95% ethyl alcohol; dilute to 70%). Dip the specimen from the alcohol to the alcohol-eosin solution. Remove immediately back to the alcohol. Repeat until visual observation shows that the internal structures have absorbed the proper amount of stain; then soak for a few minutes in the 70% alcohol. Continue the dehydration in 95% alcohol and then immerse in xylol. When clear, remove the specimen from xylol to acetone for a quick wash, blot dry and then immerse in styrene monomer for penetration.

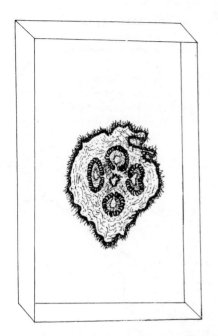 

PLATE 21. Aurelia (left) and Razor Clam (right).
Aurelia and other small transparent animals are easily stained by the eosin dip staining method described in Paragraph #15, page 52.

Labels may be made by using India ink or a typewriter and embedding them in the plastic block with the specimen (as shown above) or may be attached to the outside of the block with cellophane tape. When embedding labels, they should be placed on the base layer and allowed to set well before pouring the second layer to prevent floating out of place. They should also be soaked in styrene monomer before they are pressed against the plastic to eliminate air bubbles.

PREPARATION OF LIZARDS AND
AMPHIBIANS BY INJECTION METHODS

1. This method requires the use of a hypodermic syringe, but is advantageous because it shortens the time required for curing and dehydration because of the extreme penetration of solutions.

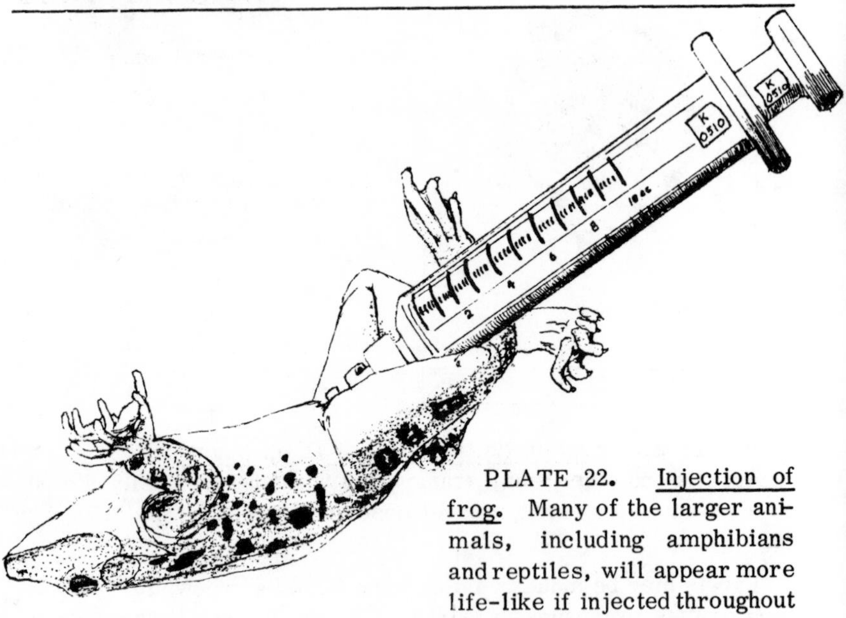

PLATE 22. Injection of frog. Many of the larger animals, including amphibians and reptiles, will appear more life-like if injected throughout the entire process as described in the techniques explained in this chapter.

The specimen shown on the next page, a horned lizard, Phrynosoma coronatum, 75 millimeters in length, was killed by abdominal injection of 10 milliliters of 50% ethyl alcohol through the vent. The lizard was then mounted on cardboard and submerged in CME F3 preservative. The injection was made with a 10 milliliter hypodermic syringe fitted with a #20 needle. The needle was inserted into the vent and then pushed through the wall of the cloaca and deep inside the body cavity. This allows the liquid to be injected and trapped within the abdomen where its only escape is through penetration of the body wall. The wall of the abdomen was fully distended. The specimen was left in CME F3 for two weeks. At the end

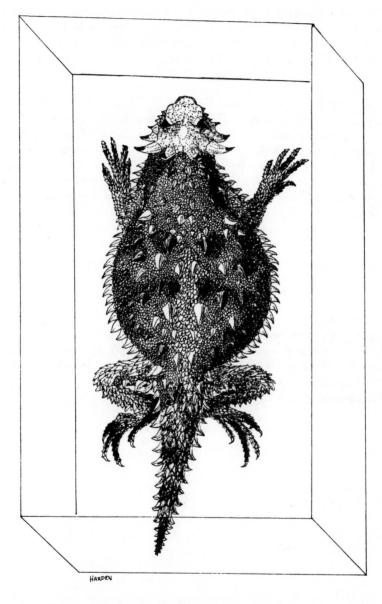

PLATE 23.   Plastic Mount of Horned Lizard.   The above lizard was treated as described in paragraph #1 on page 54. Note the full, life-like appearance of the entire specimen.

of the curing period the body wall had wrinkled heavily. The lizard was removed from the preservative and allowed to drain on paper towels. A second injection was made using ethylene glycol and the fluid was then drawn out with the hypodermic after a half hour. Flushing the cavity was repeated in the same manner many times. When the glycol that was removed from the cavity was no longer milky, fresh glycol was injected and the entire animal was submerged in ethylene glycol overnight. The following day the animal was removed to paper towels and the glycol inside of the body cavity was removed with the syringe. (Always use the vent for entrance to the body when using a hypodermic needle.) The cavity was next flushed with several washings of acetone and finally with styrene monomer. NL 600 Plastic, with an equal part of styrene monomer was catalyzed with one drop of catalyst per ounce and injected inside the abdominal cavity. The entire animal was submerged in styrene monomer for twelve hours; then drained and mounted.

On this animal some of the scale caps became loose and had to be removed. This did not affect the appearance of the finished specimen.

A repetition of the same technique was made with another lizard, Uta stansburiana, the Brown-shouldered Lizard. The initial cure was reduced to one week because of the smaller size. Otherwise the above technique was carefully followed and the results were excellent. The same procedure should be adaptable to amphibians and to fish as well.

SOME FINAL SUGGESTIONS

1. A Polyester Embedding Medium for Sectioning.

Sectioning of animal specimens means cutting up a definite part of the body with a sectioning knife (used in most biological laboratories) into thin sections in which the various details can be seen clearly. If the part of the animal to be sectioned is first embedded in clear plastic, the plastic acts as an effective support. After cutting a thin section may be placed on a microscope slide, or may be re-embedded in a thin plastic mount. The following is abstracted from <u>Stain Technology</u>(33-1) by permission of Natcol Laboratories.

Abstract: - A modified polyester resin, designated as C. M. E. Tissue Support Resin can be cut on a rotary microtome and can yield sections from 5 to 50 in number from tissue blocks that range from 5 to 16 millimeters in diameter. It is firm enough to support hard structures that lie adjacent to soft ones and retain all in their normal position. The resin-catalyst-promoter system cures or hardens at low temperature so that the blocks are ready for cutting six hours after the tissue has been routinely dehydrated.

The resin is compounded from a plasticized, rigid polyester and adjusted to proper viscosity. Several grades of hardness can be attained by adjusting the formula. It has been tested with both soft and hard tissues, including limbs and tails of 7-month old mice and mature whole grains of wheat, and provides a more substantial and more readily prepared embedding medium than celloidin. Sections can be stained before mounting, without removing the embedding material, with aqueous safranin O followed by fast green FCF in absolute (100%) alcohol. The plastic remains clear. Other staining processes require modifications to get good results.

(The above research was done in the field by Geraldine D. Kuhn and Earnest L. Lutz, Sr.).

2. Procedure for using C. M. E. - TSR Embedding Resin.

    a. Materials and equipment.
       Resin is supplied in three grades including the catalyst-promoter chemicals.
       20 or 30 milliliter beakers.
       5 or 6 milliliter glass stirring rods.
       Gelatin capsules No. 000 to 10, depending on the size of specimens to be mounted.

Mold holder made by pouring melted paraffin around inverted caps of capsules to be used.

Low vacuum chamber.   This can be made by attaching a small water faucet-operated pump to the side arm of a large mouth erlenmeyer filter flask.

On the most resistant tissues a pressure chamber may also be needed.

b. Procedure.

Fix tissue by any routine micrological method.

Wash tissue thoroughly in running water.

Dehydrate tissue by the alcohol series method.   Use two changes of absolute ethyl alcohol.

Place tissue in anhydrous ether for two to four hours.

Remove ether-saturated tissue to partially catalyzed resin for penetration.

Fill capsules with fully catalyzed resin and place tissues inside capsules.   Allow to harden.

c. Microtome sections are cut from the block in the usual manner.

d. Staining is done without removing the sections from the thin slice of resin which supports them.   Many of the ordinary stains have been used.   Overstaining is seldom encountered if the staining time is increased, but tissues may be destained by the usual method.

e. Mount sections, using cover-glasses attached to the slides with permount (a clear, cementing compound).

(The above instructions are in outline form and more complete details are shipped with the resin from the manufacturer.)

3.   Many of the smaller animals, such as insects, larva or pelagic forms of marine invertebrates, are too small to be mounted in standard blocks.   Such specimens are valuable if mounted on slides and with cover-glasses.

Curing is best accomplished in small dishes, using AFA or Gilson's fluid.   Ten or twelve hours is usually sufficient to effect a good cure.   Transfer the specimens to ethylene glycol for six hours and then place in acetone.   Using a medicine dropper flush each animal with acetone; then allow to soak two or three hours.   Drain off the excess acetone on clean absorbent paper tissue and then transfer to styrene monomer.   After four hours transfer the specimens to a fresh solution of styrene monomer.

Prepare a sheet of glass by cutting strips of heavy cardboard and taping them to the glass so that they form a very shallow box the thickness of the cardboard. Fill this with catalyzed fast-setting resin and place the specimens in the resin so that they can be cut apart into small blocks that will mount on a glass slide. When the plastic is almost dry, score it with a sharp knife or razor blade so that it will be easily cut when hard. Finish the cure until thoroughly dry and then place in warm detergent water until the plastic sheet separates from the glass. Finish cutting out the squares and mount.

4. Each mount prepared for serious study should be tagged with genus and species names and locality where collected. It is also advisable to include the common name of the animal and the name of the collector. These tags may be printed with India Ink and embedded with the animal or may be attached to the edge of the mount by use of cellophane tape. (See illustration of this on page 53.) The latter has its advantages in that errors may be easily corrected and keying of the animals may be done leisurely and in spare time. Some references are included in the bibliography which may be useful in classification.

It is further suggested that a card index system may be used in the following manner. Prepare cards for each mount to include ecological data (that is type of plant community or habitat where the animal is found) or other important information. File these cards and they will be available to use for display purposes whenever the mounts are placed out for public exhibition.

5. This book can do no more than suggest the great scope of embedding in polyester plastic resins. At a later date it is hoped that a revision will include more complete information and newer methods, but until that time it is the desire of the author that many people will find instruction and pleasure through experimenting with the plastic embedding of animals as suggested in this book.

SOME OTHER PLASTICS SUPPLIERS

The resins produced by the following manufacturers are presently being tested by the author and are presumed, until proved otherwise, to be good quality for embedding:

American Handicrafts Company, Box 791, Fort Worth, Texas.
  (Producers of "Clear-plas.")

Plastic Products Company, P.O. Box 1415, Salt Lake City, Utah.
  (Producers of "Lam-a-cast.")

SUGGESTED REFERENCES

General

Bauer, Alfred. Laboratory Directions for Histological Techniques. University of Kentucky, 1955.

Conn, H. J. 1953. Biological Stains. Bioteck Pub., Geneva, N. Y.

Cowdry, E. V. 1948. Cartilage and Cartilagenous Skeleton, Laboratory Techniques in Biology and Medicine. William and Williams Co., Baltimore, Md.

Dawson, A. B. 1939. Visualization of the Vertebrate Skeleton in the Entire Specimen by Clearing and Selective Staining. American Biology Teacher, 1, 91-93.

Edwards, J. J. and M. J. 1959. Medical Museum Technology. Oxford Univ. Press, London, England.

Fessenden, G. R. 1949, Preservation of Agricultural Specimens in Plastics. U. S. Dept. of Agric., Misc. Pub., 679, Washington D. C.

Guyer, Michael F. 1953. Animal Micrology. Univ. of Chicago Press.

Lutz, Earnest L., Sr. Embedding and Laminating with CME-D Series Polyester Resins, 1960, Natcol Products, P. O. Box 227, Redlands, California.

Pantin, D. F. A., 1946. Notes on Microscopical Techniques for Zoologists, Cambridge Univ. Press, London, England.

Peck, J. M. and D. R. Gray. 1948. A Simplified Technique for Preservation of Anatomical Specimens in Plastic. American Journal of Clinical Pathology, 18, 910-12.

Sprecht, Randolph. Preservation of the Color and Shape of Flowers. Bulletin Series No. 40, Univ. of Florida Press.

Wards Inc., 1950. How to Embed in Bioplastic. Wards Natural Science Establishment, Rochester, New York.

Taxonomy and Ecology

Abbott, R. Tucker. 1954. American Sea Shells. D. Van Nostrand Company, Inc., New York.

Barbour, Thomas. 1926. Reptiles and Amphibians, Their Habits and Adaptations. Houghton Mifflin Co.

Brown, Vinson and Henry Weston, Jr. 1961, Handbook of California Birds. Naturegraph Co., Healdsburg, Calif.

Burt, William H. and Richard P. Grossenheider. 1952. A Field Guide to the Mammals. Houghton Mifflin Co.

Conant, Roger. 1958. A Field Guide to the Reptiles and Amphibians. Houghton Mifflin Co. (Covers eastern North America.)

Essig, Oliver W. 1958. Insects and Mites of Western   North
America. Macmillan Co.

Ditmars, Raymond L. 1936. Reptiles of North America, Revised
Edition. Doubleday and Co.

Hedgpeth, Joel. 1961. Common Seashore Life of Southern California. Naturegraph Co., Healdsburg, Calif.

Keen, Myra A. 1958. Sea Shells of Tropical West America. Stanford Univ. Press.

Light, S. F. 1957. Intertidal Invertebrates of the Central California Coast. Univ. of California Press, Berkeley, Calif.

Lutz, Frank E. 1935. Field Book of Insects, Putnam.

Michener, Charles D. and Mary H. 1951. American Social Insects.
D. Van Nostrand .Co.

Miner, Roy Waldo. 1950. Field Book of Seashore Life. Putnam.

Needham, J. G. and J. T. Lloyd. 1937. The Life of Inland Waters.
Comstock Publishers, Ithaca, N. Y.

Pennak, R. W. 1953. Fresh-water Invertebrates of the United
States. Ronald, New York.

Peterson, Roger Tory. 1947. Field Guide to the Birds. Houghton
Mifflin.

Peterson, Roger Tory. 1961. Field Guide to Western Birds, Revised Edition. Houghton Mifflin.

Pratt, H. S. 1935. A Manual of the Common Invertebrate Animals,
Revised Edition. Blakiston, Philadelphia.

Ricketts, Edw. F. and Jack Calvin. 1952. Between Pacific Tides.
Rev. Edit. by Joel W. Hedgpeth. Stanford Univ. Press.

Savage, Jay. 1960. An Illustrated Key to the Lizards, Snakes and
Turtles of the West, Revised Edition. Naturegraph Co.

Smith, Lynwood. Common Seashore Life of the Pacific Northwest.
1962. Naturegraph Co.

Smithsonian Institution. 1944. A Field Collector's Manual   in
Natural History. Smithsonian Institute.

Stebbins, Robert C. 1954. Amphibians and Reptiles of Western
North America. McGraw-Hill Book Co., N. Y.

Yonge, C. M. 1949. The Sea Shore. Collins, London.

INDEX

Do not circulate

S
529
R0143655496   SSC   H259

HOUSTON PUBLIC LIBRARY

CENTRAL LIBRARY
500 MCKINNEY